Work from Home Opportunities

Home Based Job Ideas For Business, How To Make A Living From Anywhere, An Easy Guide With A Successful List Of Jobs

CYRIL EVERILL

© **Copyright 2019 - All rights reserved.**

The content contained within this book may not be reproduced, duplicated or transmitted without direct written permission from the author or the publisher.

Under no circumstances will any blame or legal responsibility be held against the publisher, or author, for any damages, reparation, or monetary loss due to the information contained within this book, either directly or indirectly.

Legal Notice:

This book is copyright protected. It is only for personal use. You cannot amend, distribute, sell, use, quote or paraphrase any part, or the content within this book, without the consent of the author or publisher.

Disclaimer Notice:

Please note the information contained within this document is for educational and entertainment purposes only. All effort has been executed to present accurate, up to date, reliable, complete information. No warranties of any kind are declared or implied. Readers acknowledge that the author is not engaging in the rendering of legal, financial, medical, or professional advice. The content within this book has been derived from various sources. Please consult a licensed professional before attempting any techniques outlined in this book.

By reading this document, the reader agrees that under no circumstances is the author responsible for any losses, direct or indirect, that are incurred as a result of the use of the information contained within this document, including, but not limited to, errors, omissions, or inaccuracies.

Table Of Contents

Introduction 1

Chapter 1: Taking Control Of Your Life By Taking Control Of Your Finances 5

    Bad Money Habits You Should Avoid 6

    Good Money Habits To Develop 11

    Making The Most Of Your Time 19

    Self-Discipline 22

    Positive Thinking And Your Success 24

Chapter 2: Training Yourself To Work At Home (Offline/Online) 27

    The Skills You Must Have 28

    Working With The Skills You Have 30

    Basic Skills You Need To Work From Home 32

    How You Can Acquire New Skills 35

    Helpful Tools 37

Chapter 3: Get a move on! - Effective Ways on Finding Job Opportunities 40

    How To Start Finding The Work You Want To Do 41

    Techniques To Get Hired 43

Chapter 4: How Are Online Jobs Paid? 47

    Your Pay Rate 49

    You Get to Decide Who You Become - Online Jobs You Can Choose From 50

Chapter 5: Work At Home Options For You 53

Freelance Writing-... 53

Proofreading-Editing... 56

Virtual Assistant 59

Web Search Evaluator 62

Website Tester-... 64

Forum/Chat Moderator- 66

Book Narrator-.. 68

Graphics Designer.. 70

Earning Money Streaming Games 73

Driving-... 74

Paid To Shop For Others 75

Providing Care In Your Home.. 76

Customer Service Representative 77

Online Tutor: Earn between $14 and $25 dollars per hour 78

Marijuana License Checker 79

Photography-.. 79

Chapter 6: Micro-jobs.. 80

Taking Surveys 80

Watching Videos-... 81

Reviewing Music- 81

Playing Games- 81

Earn Money Searching The Internet- 82

Read Emails-... 82

Uploading Receipts- *83*

Viewing Ads On Your Phone- *85*

Test Apps- *85*

Mystery Shopping- *85*

Creating Lists- *86*

Writing Reviews- *86*

Accepting Gigs- *87*

Lose Weight- *88*

Create An Online Course- *88*

Rent Out A Room- *89*

Participate in Market Research- *89*

Investing In The Stock Market- *90*

Teach- *90*

Become A Life Coach- *91*

Blogging *92*

Chapter 7: At Home Businesses **98**

Spotting Scams **113**

Conclusion **117**

Introduction

Working from home is something that most people only dream of. It is a major decision that requires a lot of research as well as planning. For many people this makes them feel out of their reach. This book is going to show you that it is entirely possible, affordable and certainly not difficult as it looks.

So many people find themselves working in the wrong place. They get up for work each morning, and instead of looking forward to going to work they dread it. They hate even thinking about their jobs. Maybe that sounds like you? Or perhaps you just feel like it is time for a change. Are you tired of going to the same job day after day and never feeling like you are getting anywhere? Maybe you simply want to experience something different, master new abilities and have free time to travel the world. Have you ever felt like you need a break from your life....and the world keeps running on independently?

Well, I have good news for you. There is a huge abundance of at-home jobs available right now to give you the experience you are looking for. Actually, this is the best time to start, believe it or not, you could find something as early as today!

If you have struggled in the past or if you have decided that it is time for you to take control of your life, you can work from the comfort of your chair and earn a great income doing so. Even if you are a free spirit, just let me tell you that most of what I am about to mention, can be easily applied from anywhere in the world! Do not limit yourself in your house if you don't feel like to do it.

Working remotely allows you to finally have control over your own schedule. You get to be in charge of your days instead of allowing other people to tell you when and how you will work. Do you love staying at home? Only want to work when the kids are at school? Did you recently have a new baby and are afraid to leave them with a sitter? Working as a freelancer will allow you to be with your baby all day long.

When you work remotely you are going to have more time to do the things that you have always wanted to do. Most people find that when they break away from traditional jobs, they have more free time to spend with family and friends.

All of us have the ability to take the thing that we love and turn it into an income when we decide to take control of our lives. You won't find yourself dreading work when you are doing what <u>you</u> really like.

When you decide to become self-employed at home it means no more commuting, no more struggling to schedule appointments around work, no more worrying about taking a day off if your kids are sick, and no more getting stuck in the traffic.

When you work from home you are the one in charge.

This book is a very simple guide written to give the readers a general idea of the types of jobs that are available nowadays. It is up to you to go deeper into some of these opportunities and make the first step. Because there is an infinite number of possibilities when it comes to working at home, each of the jobs in this manual includes a short description in order to help motivate you to find the perfect work at home job for you. Simply searching for the job title will result in hundreds of possible jobs.

Even if you do not have any budget to start with, you will find something that you can do to make money from home in this book.

While the majority of the jobs in this book can take place inside your home, some will require you to go out of your comfort place.

This book is for anyone who is wanting to make a fresh start or who wants to makean additional income. In this book, you will find jobs that you can do in your spare time or jobs that you can do full time from the comfort of your own home.

Be aware that some of the info might change over time, as companies, web sites and rules constantly change, So make sure you check properly before apply anywhere.

I, myself tried several jobs from the list, although the majority came from people I had the chance to interview and they were kind enough to share with me their experience

Countless opportunities are waiting for you out there. This list's purpose is to make you realize how vast is the work panorama right now, don't be afraid to rethink your life.

Note: Inside this book, you will find many websites, but in the paperback version it's not possible to click over them. Hence there won't be any links, if you wish to receive the complete list of web links for free, simply write to cyrileverill@mail.com, thank you!

Chapter 1: Taking Control Of Your Life By Taking Control Of Your Finances

It is very easy for us to allow money to control our lives. It happens without us even realizing it that is something that none of us can live without and while many of us would like to think that we are in control of our finances, often that is not the case. Most of us struggle with money at one point or another in our lives. Many people find, however, that their problems stem from their inability to take control of their finances. They spend money without thinking about the consequences, lack savings, and end up suffering when they could be thriving.

Money is a very important part of all of our existences. However, it should never be the most important part of your life. It is nothing more than a tool that we have, which we can use to obtain the things that we want in our lives. When money becomes the most important part of our lives it begins to control us instead of us controlling it.

What many people do not understand, or they fail to realize is that by taking control of their finances, they can have a much happier, stress-free life, while being able to do what they love.

Bad Money Habits You Should Avoid

Habits are the things that we do over and over again without ever having to think about them. They are tough to break and not all of them are good for us. Bad habits can cause you to have to deal with a lot of stress in your life. This is why it is very important for you to learn how to interrupt them. Only by breaking bad routines that you currently have will you be able to take control of your finances.

1. Spending More Money Than You Are Earning- One of the worst things that you can do for your finances is relying on credit cards to cover the extra expenses. As you continue your credit card debt goes up, payments increase, and you struggle even more. Often times, this leads to late or even missed payments which will affect your credit even more.

If you are spending more than what you are making right now, this is the very first thing that you are going to need to address. You see, in order to be able to begin freelancing, you are going to need to be in control of your finances as you grow your home business or as you transition from working outside of the home. Living within your means is vital to this process. There are two different things that you can do if you are spending more than what you are earning. You can cut your spending and learn how to budget better. (We will talk about budgeting a little bit later.) Or you can figure out new ways to earn more money and be sure you are not spending more than enough.

If you are using your credit cards to cover the basic necessities in your life such as rent, food, or other bills, or if you are purchasing items mindlessly using your credit cards, you need to take control of the situation immediately.

While there are times in your life that you are going to have to rely on credit, such as when you are purchasing a home, you should never use it to cover your bills. If you are doing this, you need to stop right now.

2. Using Payday Loans - Something that you should NEVER use. The interest is far too high for anyone to be paying and payday loans can end up creating a vicious cycle of borrowing and paying that you will never be able to get out of.

3. Lacking An Emergency Fund- Have you ever had something happen, for example, your tire blows out on your car and you didn't have enough money to replace it? Things happen in life and it is very important for us to be prepared for them to happen. We have to understand that in life things don't always go right and when they do go wrong, we need to be able to ensure that we are financially prepared.

No one ever wants to be caught off guard, especially when it comes to their finances. This is why it is so important for you to start an emergency fund right now. An emergency fund can start off small but make sure that you are contributing to it regularly in order to build up at least three months' worth of your income. This is going to ensure that no matter what happens, you will have enough money to handle it.

4. Not Paying Your Bills On Time- When you don't do it on time, you have to pay late fees. These late fees add up over time. For example, if I were to pay my electric bill late, I would have to pay a 15 dollar fee. What if I paid my electric bill late every single month for a year? I would end up paying $180 in late fees! There are a lot of

other things that I would rather do with that $180 than spend it on late fees.

On top of late fees, if you pay your bills late, such as your car payment or your mortgage payment it is going to be reported to the credit bureaus and your credit score is going to go down. This is going to cost you money in the future because when you apply for a loan you are going to be charged higher fees due to your lower credit score.

The best thing that you can do is to make sure that you are paying your bills on time. If you are the type of person that puts things off till the last minute or simply forgets when bills are due, enrol in auto-pay. This is going to save you a ton of money in late fees and it is going to ensure that your credit score does not drop.

5. Not Having A Savings Account- We already talked about an emergency fund, however, having a savings account is important as well. You have to make sure that you are saving for your future. You don't want to end up 80 years old and having to go to work every day because you did not plan for the future. There are plenty of low-risk options that you can use to grow your money and build your wealth.

6. Not Taking Responsibility Over Your Job- Do you go to a job every day that you hate? Or perhaps you don't have a job at all? You have to take responsibility for the career you choose. You are taking steps toward improving yourself by reading this book and learning how you can work at your place doing what you love, and that is a great start. It can be scary at first when you decide to make a career change or to start a new business. You have to put yourself out there and take risks. You need to remember though that the outcome is completely up to you.

When you are done the reading, what you do with the information that you learn is going to be completely up to you. If you are willing to put in the work, you will see great changes in your life. However, if you read the book and expect things to work out without putting any work into them, things in your life are going to remain the same.

7. Blaming Others- We all know that life is not fair. Chances are that you have said this to yourself or to someone else more than a few times. It is true. Life is not fair. Not all of us are given the same opportunities as others, not all of us have a rich uncle that is going to leave us everything, and not all of us have someone we can depend on to make up the difference if our checks are a little short.

Blaming others is not going to help you financially though. You have to start by accepting that you are in the situation that you are in and you must decide to make the best of it. Comparing yourself to others is only going to cause you to feel depressed. Instead, compare yourself to you. Are you better off financially this year than you were last? Where are you going to be next year?

8. Making Excuses- Stop allowing excuses to hold you back financially. You have the ability to take control of your finances as well as your life if you will just stop making excuses. Change the way that you think about money, change your spending habits, stop taking so much time off of work, or start working more. Do not allow excuses to take away your happiness in life.

When it comes to avoiding such things, it is often much easier for a person to break a bad habit by replacing it with a good one. That is why it is so important for you to create a new reality, follow me in the next section as we are going to discuss it.

Good Money Habits To Develop

So many people go through life without ever developing good money habits. They live paycheck to paycheck, barely able to make ends meet. If they succeed in developing a sustainable recovery plan though, they would find that their life would be much more pleasant, and they would have much less stress.

1. Stop Impulse Buying and start mindful spending- It is so easy when you go into the store to pick up a random item and decide that you want to purchase it. This could be as simple as purchasing items at the grocery store that you did not plan for and do not need, to grabbing a fast food meal on the way home from work, to suddenly deciding that you want a new car.

We are put in situations every single day where we can spend money. Even when we are just driving from one place to another we are faced with temptation. We pass fast food places, gas stations, or favourite shopping centres and so much more. When we are feeling poorly about our lives we are tempted to go out and purchase something to make us feel better, but this won't work for a long time.

It is important for you to stop impulse buying. Try to create a list of everything that you need. You can have multiple lists. For example, when you go grocery shopping you will create a list of groceries that you need to purchase in order to create the next weeks' worth of meals. You will stick to this list and buy nothing else you don't really need.

You can set aside some money for personal purchases, or even entertainment but you want to make sure that when you reach your limit you stop spending. When you are tempted to purchase something that you have not planned for, you should ask yourself if you really have to and acting accordingly.

Instead, start to consider everything you do and purchase as a future investment, every single action becomes a brick to lay, in appearance insignificant, yet the most effective technique to build a strong wall and a future house. This can be mind-blowing once you repeat this process over and over for a long time, you will see your life change as never before.

2. Pay Your Debt Off- You need to stop accumulating debt. Stop using credit cards to pay your bills or for shopping therapy. Instead, focus on paying off your debt. There are many different ways that you can do this.

My favourite technique for paying off debt is this: You will start out by taking a look at all of the debt that you owe. Find the one that is the smallest. For example, if you owe, $10,000, $4,000, and $1,000 in credit card debt you are going to start with the 1,000 dollars in debt. You will pay the minimum balance for the other two debts each month. Then you are going to pay your minimum balance as well as every extra penny that you have not budgeted to something toward the $1,000 debt. As soon as that is paid off you will take all of the money that you were paying toward that debt, including the minimum payment of the $4,000 in debt and pay it toward the $4,000.

You will continue this process until all of your debt is paid off. This is the fastest and most effective way that I have found for debt to be paid off. You may find that you have to make some serious cuts while you are proceeding on this, but once you are done, you are going to free up a lot of your money, making it possible to start saving for the future and to finally take control of your finances.

3. Don't Spend Your Extra Cash- Just because you have money left over after all of the bills are paid, or you got a bonus at work, does not mean that you have to spend the money. Instead, focus on putting that money towards your savings. This is going to help you reach your financial goals much sooner.

4. Start Tracking Your Expenses- Have you ever found yourself wondering where all of your money has gone? For the next 30 days keep track of where every penny is spent. Know what the money was spent on, where, and when. This is going to help you see where you can make changes in your spending habits. You may find that you are spending a lot on that morning coffee than you thought you were, or that weekly visit to Wal-Mart is costing you a lot more than you expected.

In order to do this, you will want to keep all of your receipts and writing down all the expenses. You can use a special notebook for this. Each night, take a few moments to look over it, be honest with yourself and see if you spent your daily budget on things that you really needed.

Don't stop tracking your spending after a few days. You should create a habit out of this and that requires some effort. Even if you don't do it all of the time you should do it on a regular basis. Especially if you feel that your spending is getting out of control.

5. Review Your Bills- Have you noticed that some of your bills are costing a little more than they used to? Make sure that you are paying

attention to how much you are being charged each month. You may find, when you go over your bills line by line that you are being charged for more services than you are using. If you are not comfortable with the price of your bill, do not hesitate to call the company and try to negotiate the price or change it and start a new one.

6. Start Using Coupons- Coupons have become very popular over the past couple of years and they are a great way for you to save money on the products that you purchase. For example, if you are purchasing toothpaste, shampoo, conditioner, laundry soap, and toilet paper, there are usually coupons that you can use on those items.

You can find coupons in your local Sunday newspaper and online, It is important when you are using them that you are only doing it on the products that you would normally purchase. So many people get caught up in using those offers that they end up spending money on items that they would not normally buy simply because they have a coupon for it. Do not get caught in this trap.

If you do find a great deal, for example, oftentimes you can find deals where the items that you normally use will be free after the coupon, you can stock up on the item when it is free or when it is really cheap. Remember that sales come around every six weeks as do coupons. So, you do not need more than six weeks' worth of any product no matter how great the deal is.

7. Budgeting- It is very important for you not just to create a monthly budget but to make sure that you are sticking to that. To do this, just start by creating the budget. You will want to gather all of your bills for a month as well as any check stubs or sources of income.

Start by writing down on a sheet of paper all of your sources of income as well as the total amount of income that you get from each after all deductions are taken out.

Add the total amounts of all of the incomes together and this will give you your total monthly income.

The next thing that you will want to do is write down all of the bills, debts, and other expenses that you have each month. Make sure that you are including everything that you have to spend money on. Don't forget items such as pet food, gas for your car, groceries, or clothing. You should also include your emergency fund and your savings account in this list. Some people will also set money back each month for holidays as well as birthdays to ensure that they are not scrambling for a present when the time comes.

Add up the total of all of the expenses and take that away from the monthly income total. How much is left? If there is any money left you can then focus on budgeting it to entertainment, savings, or to pay off debt depending on your situation. If there is no money left or you find that you do not have enough money to cover your expenses, you will need to go back over your expenses and start making cuts. You will have to find places that money is being spent within your budget that you can avoid. Work your way through your budget as many times as necessary to ensure that you create one that works for you.

This is a great way for you to learn the difference between your needs and your wants. Make sure that you are providing yourself with a little flexibility by having a category labelled as miscellaneous. This category will be for expenses that do not happen every month that you tend to forget about, your kids' field trips, or other miscellaneous expenses.

What do your money habits look like right now? Do you have a lot of bad money habits that you need to replace with good money habits?

Or are you practicing mostly good money habits in your life? How could you improve your money habits in order to take control of your finances?

Making The Most Of Your Time

Time is the most valuable of all of the possessions that we could ever have. This is why it is so vital for us to make the most of it. Do you ever find that you are not getting everything done that you thought you would have in a certain time frame? Perhaps at the end of the day, you are finding that your to-do list is nowhere near done. You are not alone, today, more than ever. The following tips will help you get the most out of your time so that you no longer have to feel this way.

1. Always Schedule Time To Plan- Make sure that you are scheduling 30 minutes out of each day to plan the following day. This is going to ensure that you know exactly what needs to be done. How much time each task is going to take when each task should be completed, and what your priorities will be. Some people prefer to use the first 15 to 30 minutes of their day for planning. I prefer to start my planning the night before because it allows me to see if I have any appointments

scheduled that I need to be aware of the next morning, and it allows me time to prepare for what needs to be done.

During this time, you can create your to-do list or your schedule, you can also create your goals. It is also during this time that I will add any tasks or appointments to my planner for the following days. Using a planner is a really good idea if you want to stay on top of the tasks that you need to get done.

You may find that writing down your to-do list in a notebook is what works best for you. However, if that is not the case there are plenty of apps that you can use in order to create to-do lists each day. Evernote is one of the greatest. When you are working as a freelancer you are going to find that you have a ton of different notebooks. Evernote will allow you to cut down on the notebooks and help you to keep everything together in one place. It is also going to allow you to use all of your devices which means that you do not have to be at your desk to add a note to Evernote. You will be able to create lists with checkboxes to help ensure that you are getting everything done. There are of course plenty of other time management apps that you can use. There are apps that will help you to track the amount of time that you are spending on your tasks, those that will help you to remember everything that you need to get done, help you stay motivated, and use your time wisely.

2. Remember that there are 24 hours in each day. 8 of those hours are used for sleeping which means that you have a total of 16 hours each day that you can use. Make sure that you are planning how to use them wisely. Sit down and create a list of all of the things that you want to start getting done each day. For example, exercise, sleeping, eating, meditation, work, chores, and so on. Next to each task, write down the amount of time that you are going to dedicate to that task. Add it all up and see if you can fit it into one day. Many people find that they have more than enough time to do all of the things that they want to do.

3. Find out where time is being wasted. Many people fall victim to time-wasters, and they don't even know it. These are mindless activities that take part in each day such as, scrolling through social media, playing games on their devices, watching television, or daydreaming. There is, of course, a time and place for everything in life, however, most people do not know how to set limits on these mindless activities. Because of that, they end up wasting precious time that they could be working on something much more productive.

ToDoList - This is a great app for those that want a digital to-do list. It allows you to organize all of the tasks that you need to complete as well as prioritize them. The app will also show you how much progress you are making toward reaching your goals and you will earn points for completing your tasks.

Try to be picky, your actual situation is nothing more than your self-reflection. If you want to learn how to work from your base, you are going to have to take control of your time. It can be very tempting to sit in front of the television all day but when payday comes and there is no money, it could mean that you are headed back to working outside for someone you don't want to.

Self-Discipline

One of the most important skills that you are going to need when you decide to become self-employed is self-discipline. It is tempting to allow those projects to build up on your desk as you spend your time doing things that you have always wanted to do… Finally getting the house organized, catching up on your favourite television show, spending time with your family, or just relaxing as you scroll through your phone. If you continue to do this day after day, chances are that you are struggling with self-control. Self-discipline is the ability to overcome how you feel and do what you know needs to be done no matter how big the temptations, not to do those things, are.

Learning this precious discipline is going to come down to one thing and that is the mindset. The first step is to define what your goals are as well as your motivation behind them. Take the time to write your goals down as well as why you want to accomplish them in the first place. If your reason for wanting to achieve your goals is not strong enough you are going to have a very hard time staying motivated.

Before you begin you must decide that you are not going to allow yourself to give up. It is very easy to give up when you face challenges as you work toward your desires. However, giving up is not something that a self-disciplined person would do. Deciding ahead of time that you are going to do whatever it takes to reach your target is going to help ensure that you do not give up.

Self-discipline can be achieved by creating a plan. Know what you are going to do in your mind before you take a physical step and try to enjoy the process that follows.

While it is significant for you to hold yourself accountable it is also crucial to make sure that you are not dwelling on the mistakes that you make. We all make mistakes in life. Do not allow one failure to hold you back. Instead, focus on getting back on track and learning from your mistake.

Positive Thinking And Your Success

As I stated earlier, your success is dependent upon your mindset. If you have a negative mindset as you go into your endeavor of working from home, chances are that you are going to have undesirable results.

Start each morning with positive affirmations. The way that you start your morning is going to set the tone for the rest of your day. Have you ever woken up late, felt panicked or suddenly found yourself in a bad mood? When this happens, bad things likely seem to happen all day. The reason for this is because you have started your morning out in the wrong mindset. Each morning when you wake up, start by telling yourself, "This is going to be a great day. I am going to be productive. I am going to accomplish all of my tasks today. I am going to remain focused and present. Nothing is going to stand in my way."

This may seem a little strange at first and that is okay. The more that you do it the easier it is going to be. The great thing about this technique is that you do not have to speak the words out loud. You can simply repeat them to yourself as you are getting ready for work in the morning. Be aware this won't fix your issues, that is your task.

Spend your time focusing on the good things that happen to you instead of the bad things. It does not matter how small the good things are, when you focus on the good, more good will come. If something bad does happen, try to find the humor in it. Don't allow it to drag you down or make you feel bad. Allow yourself to laugh at your mistakes and move on with your life and take it easy.

Most importantly, you should stop with the negative self-talk and replace it with positive ones. Have you ever noticed the running conversation in your mind, such as having constant intrusive obsessive thoughts? When you look into the mirror in the morning, it is the words that you think about the way that you look, the words that you say to yourself when you make a mistake, or when you face a challenge. Sadly, the majority of people take part in negative self-talk and never think twice about it. If you find yourself taking part in negative self-conversation, make a point of stopping the thought before you finish it and replacing it with positive self-talk.

For example: "There is no way that I can get all of this done." Replace it with, "I am capable of getting all of this work done because I am dedicated, self-disciplined, and persistent. Nothing is going to stop me" and so on.

By following the information in this chapter, you are going to be prepared to start working remotely. Preparing yourself before you start working from home is extremely important if you want to be successful. By taking control of your finances, and taking control of your life, you are going to allow yourself the freedom to become your own boss.

Chapter 2: Training Yourself To Work At Home (Offline/Online)

Most people have at one point or another dreamed about quitting their job and spending their days working from the comfort of their own home. The majority of people are spending hours commuting back and forth to work each day. Even if they love their job, they may struggle with the amount of time that they spend traveling back and forth to work.

When they think about working from their home, they think about sitting on the couch with their laptop in their lap, the television on in front of them, while they are curled up in their pajamas. They dream about getting up at 10 in the morning, having the freedom of taking a nap whenever they want, running errands when they see fit, meeting up with their friends for lunch, and enjoying a life of luxury.

Working remotely means that you are spending the majority of your time alone. There will be no people stopping by your desk in the middle of the day for a chat, but there will be many distractions and no one to controls you, so it's imperative maintaining the right determination and stay focused in order to accomplish multiple tasks.

Of course, this is not to say that working as a freelancer does not come with its perks. Freelancing can be wonderful if you have the will that it takes.

The Skills You Must Have

A good place to start is having a solid command of basic life skills, but there are certain ones that you must have if you want to work long term, no matter what field that you are in. Without these abilities, working remotely may prove to be more challenging than it is worth.

1. The ability to focus completely on what you are working on. If your phone rings, if the washing machine needs to be changed, if the dog is barking, if someone knocks on your door, you need to be able to ignore them in order to make sure that you are getting your work done. You can't scroll through Facebook for just a couple of minutes and then get back to work. When you go to your desk, you have to concentrate on what you're doing in the same way that you would if you were at the office. Of course, you can schedule breaks just like you would have at work and with that time you can do whatever you need. The point is though that you have to treat your work at home

the same way that you would any other profession and you have to make sure that you are well focused.

2. Organization is extremely significant as well. When you go to your regular job right now, chances are that you keep your desk nice and organized. However, when you are at home it is very easy to fall victim to clutter. You want to make sure that you are keeping your working area organized by having a dedicated space. When your workday is done, you will leave after you have cleaned. Organization is also important when it comes to ensuring that you do not get your orders confused. If you are managing multiple clients, make sure you do not miss any deadlines, spending a few dollars on a good planner is great to guarantee your results. It will also help not overbooking yourself, which can happen a lot when you are first starting out.

3. Being able to spend large amounts of time alone might be tricky, while for some people it comes very natural When you first start working as a freelancer, chances are that you are going to miss being around people. You may want to consider growing a balance between yourself and healthy social interaction.

4. Having the ability to motivate yourself is also extremely important. When you are working from home, you don't have to worry about your boss walking in while you binge-watch Netflix or scroll through social media. You don't have to worry about getting in trouble for doing the laundry or taking the day off. However, if you are unable to stay motivated you will continue to put work off and never get it done. Schedule your days off. Plan for home chores and other activities outside of your work hours. Work, during your work hours and do everything else during another time period. This is vital to your success.

Working With The Skills You Have

Later in this book, as we go through the different types of jobs that are available for you to do at home, you may start to feel a bit overwhelmed. You may feel like you have no idea where to start or what job you should be doing.

I want to provide you with a little bit of encouragement because it is possible for you to start right now, without acquiring more skills.

I want you to take some time and think about the skills that you currently possess. If you want to get started working for yourself right away, it is best if you begin from the abilities that you already possess.

Take a few moments and write everything down. What are you good at? Do you have specific technical skills that will help you find a job at home? As we go through the different types of work at home jobs, later on in this book, think about the skills that are required and ask yourself if you can master some. Those jobs would be the best place for you to start.

You may want to think about something that you enjoy doing as you go through the list when you are earning at your place, It can be very tough to stay motivated to complete work when you do not have a boss looking over your shoulder if you do not appreciate the work that you are doing. On top of that, if you love what you do, you won't feel like working at all. You can expect yourself to produce better results this way, meaning also, you will be able to find clients more easily having an increase in demand.

When you focus on using the skills that you already have there are going to be plenty of opportunities for you to start making money from home right away.

Basic Skills You Need To Work From Home

There are so many different types of freelance jobs available that anyone can find one that will work for them. However, you may feel that you don't currently possess the skills that you need in order to achieve that. Before we go into the different places where you can learn these skills let's go over a few basic skills that you are going to need no matter what field you go into.

1. Microsoft Office- If you are not currently familiar with Word, PowerPoint, and Excel you are going to want to make sure that you take the time to learn about it before you start working as a freelancer. Many of the jobs that you will be applying for are going to use Microsoft Office in one way or another. Knowing how to navigate and work with Microsoft Office is going to open up many at home job opportunities to you. You can find courses on Microsoft office at your local library, a local community college, or online. Most of these courses are going to be free.

2. Google Suite- Free and paid plans. Services as Gmail, Google Drive, and all of the other Google products, allow documents to be shared between clients and their contractors. You are going to find as

you start freelancing that many clients use Google and expect that you know how to use it as well. Again, there are many courses online that you can take for free a learn how to use Google products.

3. Grammar- Using good grammar when you write and when you speak is going to help you to make a good impression with your potential clients. It is also important if you want to work in any type of job that involves words.

4. Basic computer skills- Freelancing means that if there is a problem with your computer, your WIFI, your network, or your software, you are the one that has to figure it out. Technical problems will arise at one point or another in your freelancing career. Chances are they are going to happen more often than you would like. You have to be able to deal with the most common issues and find answers when you don't know what to do. Being able to fix the problem as soon as possible so that you can get back to work.

5. Focus on your typing speed- A lot of at-home jobs require you to spend a big portion of time typing. If your typing speed is very slow you will spend a lot of extra hours working. You can easily improve your typing speed on your own and there are plenty of online

resources to help you as well. When it comes to improving your typing speed the key is repetition. You have to make sure that you are practising until you are able to move your fingers as if they are one with the keyboard. When your typing speed increases, you will experience a more excellent flow.

6. Communication - This is extremely important when you are working with multiple clients all over the world and you have to be able to communicate with each other. There are times when comprehension can be difficult due to language barriers, however, knowing how to communicate effectively can reduce these difficulties.

7. Bookkeeping skills- Tracking of all of your income as well as any expenses that you have for your business is the best way to keep control over your business, certainty, not a complicated task, but essential to pay your taxes when the time comes.

8. Marketing- If you are going to start your own business or are planning on working for yourself you are going to need to make sure that you are able to advertise yourself and your businesses to the right people. There are plenty of online marketing courses available that

can help you learn how to market your business, or you may decide to pay a professional.

9. Planning- Basic but essential skill to keep in mind. Without proper scheduling, any business can lack organization. Make sure how to create a growth plan, focusing your goals, and completing tasks each day.

How You Can Acquire New Skills

There are hundreds of different ways for you to acquire new exciting skills to level you up, depending upon the targeted job. Before we go further into discover new jobs, let's explore together a few places where you can find some knowledge.

1. The local library- Your local library may provide free courses, have a chat with the librarian and find out what different courses are offered. You can also find plenty of manuals there, perfect to help you acquire new abilities as well. This is especially good if you are able to teach yourself.

2. Coursera provides more than 2,700 different courses all of which are available online. Some of the courses that are available on

Coursera are backed by different universities while others are created simply to help you learn a new skill.

3. <u>Creative Live</u>- This platform provides live classes taught by top experts in the fields. Instructors such as Victoria Will from the New York Times and Tim Ferriss can be found on this platform.

5. <u>Udemy</u>- This is a platform that provides many different types of online courses. There are paid courses as well as free courses which you can use to learn the skills that you will need in order to be a successful freelancer.

6. <u>YouTube</u> - If there was ever a place where you could learn anything it is YouTube. Simply go to the YouTube website and type in what you want to learn (such as "how to write books") into the search bar and you will get hundreds if not thousands of tutorials. YouTube is one of the best places for a person to learn a skill if they do not have any extra money to invest.

7. <u>WikiHow</u> - The paradise of written guides. Simply go to the website, type in what you want to learn and choose from hundreds of results.

Of course, this is a starting point. I created this list to give you an idea of the options that are available to you and to remind you that you can learn anything you wish…no excuses. Do not be discouraged, remember that new abilities can only be learned if you are willing to put in the time and effort to do so.

Helpful Tools

While being self-employed can be an ideal thing, it is not for everyone. There are many factors that must be considered before you make the decision to start your business. If you decide that making money at home is right for you, there are some tools that you can use to make your life easier and to make you more efficient.

Scrivener- Scrivener is a tool that will help every writer become even better. Using scrivener allows you to keep all of your notes, thoughts, and ideas in one place. As you are writing you can make notes of topics that you want to add to your book, ensuring that you do not forget anything. Scrivener was created for long writing projects. When you use Scrivener, you can create your content in any order that you would like and then add it wherever you see fit.

Grammarly- Amazing free tool for the grammar check, it can benefit many aspects of your daily typing. Using Grammarly ensures that what you are writing whether it be an email, a social media post, or a book is written correctly. You might also choose to pay a plan if you need more professional tools from Grammarly, but the free version is perfect for a beginner.

Paymo- Paymo is an app that you can use in order to manage your time, create your schedule, track the amount of time that you work on specific jobs, and to help with billing. Using Paymo can help you deliver your projects on time to your clients which oftentimes means that you will get more work.

QuickBooks - QuickBooks makes self-employment taxes easy. This app allows you to track your mileage, keep your personal and your business expenses separate and to send as well as track your invoices. It will help you with your deductions ensuring that you are getting the most out of your tax return as well. Your receipts can also be saved on this app, so you don't have to worry about keeping all of that paper around your office. Best of all those quarterly taxes are not going to be able to sneak upon you any longer.

Bluehost - If you want to create your own website, Bluehost might be right for you. Creating a website for your at-home business might sound complicated but Bluehost makes it easy. They provide 24/7 support, marketing services, paid ad credits, and a money-back guarantee.

Wix - Is another website builder that you can use to create the perfect website. There are over 500 templates to choose from and you can customize your website so that it works for both you and your customers.

Using these apps when you are working as a freelancer is a great way to safeguard most of your time, keeping your clients happy, and protecting your business. You do not need a lot of apps, however, choosing a few will benefit your incomes and is a great way to start building a strong foundation.

Chapter 3: Get a move on! - Effective Ways on Finding Job Opportunities

A niche is a specific part of the market that you will be working in which you will specialize in, an extremely important starting point.

For example, if you were to write a blog, you would not want to write a blog on every topic possible. Instead, you would want to find one topic that you would write about on a regular basis, this would be your niche.

Your niche should be something that you are passionate about because this is going to make your work much stress-free and much more enjoyable. When you are passionate about your niche you are going to look forward to getting up each morning and when you go to bed at night you are going to feel fulfilled.

When you choose your target, it should be in an area that you have a lot of knowledge. Many people will choose a niche in an area that they are an expert in. However, you have to be careful because not everything you can think about is going to result in you earning an income.

You should focus on niche-down as specific as possible. For example, if you were to create a blog, instead of creating a blog about cars, you may decide to create one about accessories but in order to make it more specific, you may decide to write about car stereo equipment. You are going to draw in people who are looking for that particular information, saving yourself a lot of frustration as well. When your niche is too broad, it's not an easy task to cover the information as well as you would if you narrowed it down.

Discovering your sweet spot allows you to provide a very specific set of skills to your customers. Clients do not want to hire someone who claims that they can do it all because they know this is impossible. Instead, they want to pay someone to do a specific job. When you have the right skills for that particular job, you will be able to find the clients that you want to work for over and over again.

How To Start Finding The Work You Want To Do

As we work through the rest of this book, you should start thinking about the specific work that you want to build. Many times, when a person decides that they want to leave their traditional job and begin working for themselves, they have no idea how to behave. This is one of the reasons that it is so important for you to narrow down your niche.

Knowing what you want to do, how you want to spend your time as you earn your income, is going to allow you to narrow down your job search. If you were to go to Google right now and type in "Work From Home Jobs," you would get millions of results. You may find some jobs that you are interested in, but chances are you would be overwhelmed with the results. On top of that, you would find that there are a lot of scams mixed in with the real jobs.

However, if you had a precise idea, you would be able to narrow the results down and possibly find what expected. Most people are going to spend hundreds of hours looking for work at home jobs. You do not have to do this though. Later in this book, we are going to go over many different occupations that you can start doing as soon as today!

If you do decide that none of the jobs is for you, there are a few things that you can do to find the best work at home job for you. The first thing is to start reaching out to your local businesses. Many companies are hiring remote workers. You may be able to reach out to local doctors and talk to them about transcribing for them if that is something that you are interested in. Or you can talk to businesses within your niche and offer them your services.

You can also reach out to your friends and family and ask them if they have any leads on work at home jobs that you can apply for. Of course, you have the ability to search the internet if that is something that you want to do. However, I do not feel that any of this is truly necessary because I am confident that I have included enough opportunities in this book for anyone to find the perfect work for them.

Techniques To Get Hired

When it comes to working as an independent contractor, finding a job usually is not the biggest challenge that people face, it is getting hired. Employers are notorious for posting at home jobs and never getting back to any of their applicants.

Applying for a work at home job is no different than applying for any other job though. The only difference is that you may have to apply a bit more than you would if you were working in an office outside of your home. Some of the work at home jobs are going to require you to apply to work for many different clients until you build up your client base. This can be very stressful because it means that the more you apply the higher your chances of rejection are. Not everyone that you apply to work with is going to hire you, you have to get used to it, learn from it, improve your technique and be as positive as possible. The more you apply....the higher the chances of getting hired.

1. Make sure that you know what you have to offer. These jobs are going to require different skills, talents, and experience. They are just like any other job that you would apply for and should be treated as such.

2. Only apply for jobs that you are qualified to do. This may sound silly but for some reason, when people begin working as a freelancer, they start applying for jobs that they do not have the skills for. Perhaps they think that they will be able to quickly learn the basics or that the client is so desperate that they will be hired anyway. If you want to work doing a specific job and you are not qualified for it, learn what is necessary before you apply.

3. Make sure that you read the entire job description and you do exactly what the employer requests of you. If the job requests a

sample of your work, send it, if the job requests a copy of your resume, make sure that you attach it. On the other hand, if the client does not ask for a sample, don't overload their email with the extra work. Of course, if you are not reading the entire job description you may end up missing important details that could cost you the client or job.

4. Do not send a standard resume or proposal to potential clients or employers. You need to create a specific offer for each job that you are applying to. Sure, this can take a little bit of time, but it is going to increase your chances of getting hired dramatically. Don't copy-paste your opportunities.

5. Don't stop applying. You may find yourself surprised at how few potential clients or employers are going to respond to your applications or proposals. don't just wait for the client to contact you. Instead, keep looking for more. If you find that you are getting rejected or you are not getting any responses, try to figure out if you are doing something wrong. You may simply be wording your proposals incorrectly or your proposals may be getting lost in cyberspace.

Be proactive and don't let anything discourage you.

Do not allow this to stop you from applying. You will at some point find a client who is willing to give you a chance and that is going to give you the experience that you need in order to take on more clients or more work.

Many people find that self-employment is a process. You may find that you have to start using your spare time to start building your client base and learn as fast as you can. However, once you start getting regular clienteles you will begin to walk away from the 9-5 world and start setting your own schedule. It is understandable that you would want to jump in with both feet when you first decide to jump on this adventure. Many people go with this all or nothing mentality and some of them succeed. The most successful people who work remotely, are the ones that took it one step at a time and did not put themselves into a position that could hurt them financially but allowed the necessary time to grow their clients or their business.

Chapter 4: How Are Online Jobs Paid?

Have you ever found yourself wondering how you will get paid when you work online? Different companies are going to pay different ways, however, when you work online you are going to get paid online as well.

You can use the different platforms that companies pay through, link them to your bank account and transfer the money yourself. This provides you with some extra security ensuring that no one is going to be able to access your bank information.

1. PayPal - This is the most commonly used platform for transferring money and get paid. This great free tool makes you able to accept payment from all over the world. It takes 3 minutes for signing up and as soon as this is done you will be able to start receiving payments. What I love about PayPal is that you will only need to provide your email as payment data, once your bank is linked to your profile, you will no longer need to show those to clients and the process will be automatic.

2. <u>TransferWise</u> - If you want your clients to transfer money directly to your bank account, you can use this brilliant banking alternative. This borderless account has a very favourable rate compared to other traditional banks. You can have as many world currencies as you need and is a very secure platform with a strong financial background. No monthly fees and minimum balance to worry about, only a small fee for your currency conversions.

3. <u>Payoneer</u> - Similarly to Transferwise, this tool allows you to receive payments from anywhere. This means that if you are working in the US, you can accept payments from Europe, China, the UK, and other countries, without having to pay conversion fees. Payments are received very quickly, and you are usually able to access them in between 2 and 6 hours after they have been sent. Once your clients have sent you $1,000 through Payoneer, you are going to earn a $25 bonus!

4. <u>N26</u> - This free online bank was created specifically for freelancers and those working remotely. With N26, you can open a business account in order to track your business expenses, manage your cash flow, and make it easier for you to file your taxes at the end of the

year. There is no minimum deposit and you can control it directly from your smartphone.

Having this set up is going to ensure that you can start taking payments right away. You can then talk to your clients and set up other payment methods if you prefer to

Your Pay Rate

How much do you want to earn? This is a question that you are going to need to ask yourself before you start everything. Do you want to make enough to cover your bills or do you want to make enough to live comfortably? When you work at home your pay rate is almost entirely up to you. The market and you get to decide your hourly rate.

First, let's understand how much you want to make each month. Divide that number by 4 and then divide it again by the number of hours that you are going to work each week. That is going to provide you with the amount of money that you need to make per hour.

When you are figuring this amount, you will also have to add in any fees that you are charged. For example, if you are working on

UpWork, they will take 20% of your earnings. This needs to be taken into account when you are figuring your pay rate.

It is also important for you to remember that not all countries have the same currency. You need to understand the conversion rates. If a client offers to pay you 1 penny per word if you are writing an article, you need to be able to convert that into your currency. You can do this easily by typing it into Google and having it converted.

You Get to Decide Who You Become - Online Jobs You Can Choose From

Working at home has been called the way of the future. It has been said that soon, the majority of people will be working this way instead of going to the office. Right now is a great time for you to start, there are so many mind-blowing opportunities that might make you rethink your entire life.

You are the one choosing what kind of reality you want to create.

Working from home can provide you with several benefits which include:

1. You will be able to generate multiple incomes.

2. It is an affordable way to create a profit if you already have the skills needed to get started.

3. You can start today. There are plenty of work at home jobs that you can start as soon as today that are not going to require any extra skills.

4. You are going to have more independence than you would if you worked for a company.

5. The job is very flexible. You can create your own schedule, work part-time, full-time, or when you are not at your day job.

If you want to be successful at becoming a freelancer, you are going to want to choose a job that suits you as well as your goals. You want to do something that you are passionate about or at the very least interested in. The most successful work at home businesses thrived because the owner was very passionate about what they did.

There are product-based businesses that you can start right out of your home. When you start one of these businesses, you will sell something to your customers. Plenty of people make a lot of money selling their products online and locally. You may also be able to sell products that you purchased at a really low price. For example, some people will search out clearance items at end of season sales, hang on to them until the following year and sell them at a discounted price, more than tripling their investment.

Of course, since we live in the age of the internet you can also sell digital items such as books, courses, videos, planner templates and so on.

The options are countless. You can do this online or offline. For example, you may decide that you want to start a daycare in your home, perhaps you want to become a virtual assistant or a life coach. All of these jobs are service-based.

Every work at home job is going to fall within these two categories. So, the first thing you want to do is decide if you want to sell a product or a service. Then as we go through the next chapter, talking about the different types of jobs, you can pick exactly what you want to do and grow into who you want to be.

Are you enjoying this book? It would mean a lot to me having a short review on Amazon. Thank you!

Chapter 5: Work At Home Options For You

Working at home is going to provide you with financial security, especially with the constant threat of cuts and layoffs that we see. As you think about building your momentum, consider these options. These jobs are either no investment or low investment jobs that you can start doing from your home in order to supplement your income or work as much as you need.

Freelance Writing-

I am starting with freelance writing because this is probably one of the quickest ways for a person to start making money from home. You can start freelance writing with no investment at all and you can start earning an income almost immediately.

There are many different ways that you can make money at home as a freelance writer and I am going to cover each of them. Before we get into that let's talk about the qualifications. Being a freelance writer requires you to be able to write suitably. You will need to have a good understanding of English as well as grammar and spelling. The equipment that you will need is a computer and an internet connection that is reliable.

Make sure you are not just relying upon software and take the time to read what you write OUT LOUD. This is going to help you see and hear any mistakes that you have made. Always double-check with Grammarly or MS Word proofreading tool and take consideration to pay a human proofreader for a final check.

Upwork - Upwork is a great place for freelance writers to start out. It is here that you can find clients. You will create a profile, and then start bidding on jobs that are posted by the clients. After you bid on the jobs, the clients will look at your proposals. They will then contact you if they are interested in working with you. Some of them will ask for a writing sample, especially if you are just starting out, so you want to make sure that you have this ready for them. This platform, other than writing, can provide you tons of different jobs you didn't even know existed, have fun with researching and discovering new interesting ways of earning.

Freelancer - This is a freelance job board much like UpWork. You will need to create a profile and then you can bid on writing jobs.

Guru- Guru is another freelance job board that is great for writers. You will have to create a profile and then begin bidding on jobs, setting your own rates, and then start earning money!

Transcribing Audio-

A transcriptionist job is to take audio and convert it into text, simple as this. When you work at home transcribing audio, clients will provide you with the audio that they need to be transcribed, you will type it up in a document and send it back to the client. It is one of the easiest job available for starting and it is in high demand.

In order to be a transcriptionist, you will need to know how to type very quickly. The faster that you can type the more money you can make. You will also need to be able to hear well and understand accents. A lot of the time when a client sends you audio it will include a speaker with an accent.

You will need a computer, internet connection, and a headset that blocks out noise. This headset is going to make transcribing much easier for you. They can be purchased relatively cheap almost anywhere.

There are a lot of other companies that hire transcribers:

Rev - If you are just starting out, Rev is a great place to begin with. You will make between 21 and 39 dollars per audio hour that you transcribe. It is not a lot of money starting out, but it will give you the experience that you need to help you get higher-paying clients.

TranscribeMe - TranscribeMe is another great company that will hire beginner freelancers. They are going to pay around 20 dollars per audio hour and will provide you with more choice.

Proofreading-Editing

Don't want to write books for a living but still want to make a lot of money working at home? Maybe proofreading is the right job for you. Before we start talking about the different jobs available let's talk about the difference in proofreading and editing. Many people think about editing and proofreading as the same thing, however, there are very important differences between the two jobs. A proofreader's job is to focus on catching errors in spelling, grammar, formatting, and syntax. The proofreader is the last person to see the work before it is published.

An editor, on the other hand, will go through the entire document it, make changes, reorganize it, check the research, and they can completely change the document. Editors and writers will work back and forth until all of the revisions are made before the work goes to the proofreader.

There are plenty of proofreading/editing jobs out there if this is something that you are interested in doing. Writers, bloggers, and many other companies are always looking for someone to go over their work and make sure that any errors are caught before the work is published.

On average, proofreaders/editors earn about $36,000 per year working full-time. If you are able to maintain several different clients, you may be able to earn more. On the other hand, if you are just looking for something to do in your free time you could earn less.

It is a good idea for you to brush up on your grammar skills. There are plenty of free online training courses available for proofreaders as well.

EditFast - EditFast is a service where clients will submit their documents to have them proofread. You can apply at EditFast, submit your resume and then take a test. If you are hired, you will then create your own page through their web page builder and then sign a non-disclosure agreement. Once everything has been approved you will be notified of any projects that are available. They do recommend that the potential proofreader has some experience proofreading and has a background in a specific field such as medical. The potential proofreader must have strong English skills. EditFast does take 40% of the price of the project so the rate that you would make would vary depending on the project.

FlexJobs - FlexJobs is a job board specifically for telecommuting positions. There are all sorts of positions available each of them having their own specific requirements however, there are a lot of proofreading jobs listed. Some of the jobs are going to be full-time, or part-time, while others will be temporary. By using FlexJobs to look for work, you are going to be able to find a wide variety of proofreading jobs, which means that there are going to be multiple opportunities for you to apply. The great thing about FlexJobs is that each company has been screened before the job is posted so you can be sure that every job posted is a legitimate one.

ProofreadingServices - ProofreadingServices offers between 19 and 46 dollars per hour depending on what your turnaround time is. The highest-paying jobs are going to have the fastest turnaround time. In order to apply, you will begin by taking a 20-minute preliminary test. The company only hires about 1 in every 300 people who apply because their screening process is so rigorous.

Virtual Assistant

Becoming a virtual assistant is one of the easiest ways for most people to start working for themselves. A virtual assistant is a home-based professional(or a digital nomad) that offers their clients administrative support in the entire world thanks to an internet connection. What does a virtual assistant do?

Virtual assistants complete a wide variety of tasks which makes it very easy for a person to find a job in this field. Tasks could include:

Social media management

Making telephone calls

Planning events

Email

Customer services

Research via the internet.

Tech support.

Appointment scheduling

Project management

Data entry

Proofreading/Editing

Writing

Managing blogs

Bookkeeping

Marketing

And much more…

Working as a virtual assistant means that you get to choose if you create your own business or if you work for a company as an employee. It does not cost very much if anything to start your own virtual assistant business. You will need a phone for daily client calls, a computer, access to the internet, a printer with a scanner, and a website if you want to market your business, the experience will come with time and practice.

As a virtual assistant, you can make between 12 to 60 dollars per hour depending on your clients, services and abilities. If you decide that you want to run your own VA business instead of work for those listed below you will be cutting out the middleman, therefore, earning a lot more money.

24/7 <u>Virtual Assistant</u> - In order to apply you will need to submit your resume. If the HR department finds that you have skills which are required by one of the company's clients, they are going to contact you. They pay between 10 and 12 dollars per hour and the amount that you get paid will depend on your skills. Most of the time though, clients are looking for part-time virtual assistants so this would be great if you were going to apply at other companies or just wanted to work part-time.

Belay - Belay hires virtual assistants, bookkeepers, and web specialists. All you have to do to apply is go to the website and click the "Apply Now" button. You will then go through an assessment to see if you are a good fit for the company. If you are, Belay will match you with clients. You can work between 10 and 40 hours per week if you are hired depending on the needs of the client.

Fancy Hands is located in New York, however, they do hire work at home virtual assistants to use common websites as well as software, make phone calls and do internet research. All you have to do to apply is head over to the website and click on the "Apply" button. This would be a great job for those that are just starting out for this career.

Web Search Evaluator

As a web search evaluator, you will do internet searches on specific topics and then you will assess the results that you receive. You will also review the sites to ensure that they have the type of content that you are looking for. You will determine how well the sites that you visit fit within the parameters that you were searching for. You can also rank the results. This is a great job if you enjoy spending your time on your computer. You will need to have a minimum of a high school diploma or GED, have good computer skills, know how to solve problems, work independently, manage your time well, and communicate well. As a web search evaluator, you can make up to $30,000 dollars per year.

Appen hires search engine evaluators as well as social media evaluators. They hire from multiple countries, so you do not have to live in the US in order to apply to this company. Select your country from a drop-down list and then fill out a registration form. The next step is screening. Once you have completed this process you will begin working for Appen. They will send you a link to their project page where all of the jobs that you are eligible for will be listed.

Lionbridge - has many different positions open for those that want to start working at home, including internet safety evaluator, ads assessor, data analyst, and much more. In order to apply, you will simply go to the website, select your country and then you will be provided with a list of job opportunities. Once you click on the job that you are interested in, you will see whether the job is full-time or part-time, as well as the requirements. Once you have gone over all of the requirements, you will click on the link to contact Lionbridge.

A member of their recruitment team will then go over your application and contact you if they are interested in hiring you.

Profit Factory - Offers a variety of different positions for virtual assistants. Each position has its own list of experience and skills required.

Website Tester-

Anyone who has a blog, website or any type of business on the internet knows how important it is to ensure that their site is user-friendly. They understand that if they are losing visitors due to poor design, bad content, or because the visitors are unable to navigate the site, they are losing money. This is why many companies are willing to pay a lot of money to have someone review their website or their mobile app.

If you want to become a website tester you will need to be skilled in using the internet and able to speak English fluently. You will also need a computer that has a microphone, a reliable internet connection, and ensure that your web browser is updated. Each of the tests are going to take anywhere from 5 to 25 minutes and you will earn an average of 10 dollars per test.

User Testing - With User Testing you can earn up to 60 dollars per test because they are willing to pay you 10 dollars for every 20 minutes of video that you complete. You will be paid to visit the websites or the apps and then complete specific tasks while speaking out loud what you are thinking. This company can help you earn some extra money on the side. You are never going to get rich working for this company because the number of tests that you receive will depend on many different factors, for example, demographics, as well as your rating. You will be paid through PayPal 7 days after you have completed the test. All you have to do is enter your email address, complete a quick sample test and then start earning some money.

User Brain - This is a great company for those that are wanting to earn a little bit of extra money on the side. You will have to download the Chrome Extension or iOS app in order to start testing websites. Each test is going to take between 5 to 15 minutes, and you will earn 3 dollars per test. This means that the most you are going to make is $12 an hour with this company, however, that is not a bad starting rate. You will have to complete a sample test after taking a tour and reading the guide. The company will then review your video and provide you feedback on how you can improve in future tests. Once you are approved you will begin getting paid tests.

Testing websites is a great way to earn money on the side. Instead of sitting around and waiting on testing jobs to come in, you can be working on another job, earning money even when you do not have any sites to test.

Forum/Chat Moderator-

There are so many different forums, groups, or chats that are dedicated to different topics all over the internet. If these forums were left to themselves, they would become extremely chaotic. This is where a moderator comes in, they keep the forums in order.

Because there are so many of these different forums and groups online, chat moderators are in high demand. For those that are wanting to start making money at home, this could be a great source of income. Many people choose to be moderators because they are able to engage in a community that they are interested in while making some money.

When it comes to money, the average moderator will make about 15 dollars per hour but can make all the way up to 30 dollars per hour. The key to earning more is knowing how to turn social conversations into sales while ensuring that the members of the community are happy with their experience. Some of the companies are going to provide their moderators with paid training. However, you can take free courses online for marketing through Study or Udemy.

Crisp Thinking - Crisp Thinking hires social media moderators. They pay about 14 dollars per hour and have offices in the UK as well as the US. You can apply by going to their website and submitting your resume. You do not have to be part of any community or group to be hired for this position.

eModeration is a social media management company that was started in 2002. Moderators that work with eModeration make between 15 and 16 dollars per hour. The company has many different big-name clients such as Game of Thrones, Smirnoff, Maxwell House, HBO, and more. Head over to the website to apply with your resume if you are interested in any of the major brands that they work with.

Book Narrator-

Have you ever been told that people love listening to you talk or that you should try doing voice overs? Can you use your voice in many different ways? If so then you may want to consider being a book narrator. For example, if you are narrating a nonfiction book you will need to take the dry facts and make them sound interesting by putting energy behind those words. If you are narrating fiction you will need to know how to use different voices as you read the dialogue, and if you are narrating children's books you will need to know how to make silly voices so the book appeals to children.

Here technical audio equipment is required for a professional result, but nowadays you can achieve this in a much affordable way than before.

How much does it pay? How much you make is going to depend on how you negotiate your rates. Most narrators are going to be able to complete about 2-5 hours of finished audio each day. On average though, a book narrator will make about 100 dollars per finished audio hour. Once you get a little experience under your belt and your sound quality grows, you may expand out, using your voice for a radio commercial, tv commercial, movies and so on.

ACX will put you into contact with authors who have books that need to be narrated. When you work with ACX you will produce the complete audiobook. This means that it is up to you to do the whole process as well as the editing and preparing the files for the client. The audiobooks that are created via ACX are sold on Amazon, iTunes, and Audible. You can choose to get paid a couple of different ways. The first way is per finished hour of audio. This means that you are going to earn one flat rate after you have completed the entire book. The second way to get paid is through royalty sharing. This is more of a residual income type of job if you choose to get paid this way. The amount of money that you would make would, of course, depend on how well the book sells and not all books sell that well. The third way to get paid is through royalty share plus. This means that you will get a per finished hour rate as well as the royalty share. The amount that you would make per finished hour would depend on the client that you are working for, however, it is likely going to be less than if you took the flat-rate payment. This is a great place for new narrators to start and many new ones have seen a lot of success by starting off with ACX.

Fiverr has a section that is specifically for narrators. You can create as many gigs as you wish, this profession can cover several different requests depending on the client. Fiverr may not be the best place to earn the highest rates, but it is a good place for you to get some experience if you are just starting out. It is also a great way for you to let your portfolio grow.

Voices is a platform that was created for audiobook narrators to be auditioned by those that are looking for voice talent. This could be for audiobooks or other projects. There are two types of membership. The first membership is free and the second costs 499 dollars per year. If you are just starting out, you may want to give the free membership a try before you sign up to pay for anything. I am not an advocate for paying to work when there are so many companies that are willing to hire you without making you pay.

Graphics Designer

If you want to do something creative while you are earning money from home, this might be the solution you are looking for. A graphics designer is a professional in the graphic art industry, a visual concept creator, Brochures, logos, magazines, reports, advertisements, are just a few examples on what you can step into. If you want to learn how to start this profession, there are plenty of courses available online as well as offline. Udemy would be a great place for a person to start learning this.

Finding clients is the hardest part of becoming a graphic designer once you have learned the skills that you will need. But don't worry, there are plenty of platforms for you to sign up for which will ensure you have all of the clients that you will ever need.

Graphics designers are in high demand so as long as you are providing your clients with the quality work that they are looking for, you should have no problem keeping busy. Here are a few starting points.

On Site - This platform was created to cut out the middleman. Freelancers do not have a percentage taken out of their earnings like they do on other platforms. Graphics designers are matched to jobs. However, to be approved, you must have agency experience as well as client experience. You have to be able to prove this experience as well. This is simply to ensure that the clients receive what they want from the designer and no one gets ripped off in the end. This is a great site to use if you have been designing for a while and want to add on some extra clients.

99designs - This is a platform specifically for designers. You choose the type of work that you want to do and when you want to do it and they will connect you with the right clients. The rates that you will earn depend on the types of jobs that you decide that you want to work on. 99designs pays their freelancers within 3 business day, they do charge a fee. When you begin working with a new client you will be charged a 100 dollar introduction fee. 99designs spreads this fee out over the first 500 dollars that you charge the client. They charge this fee for matching you with the client. They also charge a fee for every project that you complete in order to provide freelancers with support, fraud protection, and secure payments. The fee that is charged will be based on the level of the designer. For example, entry-level designers are charged a 15% fee while top-level designers are charged a 5% fee.

Canva - This is another platform that was created for designers. You can use this website to design anything from posters to eBook covers to business cards and more. There are three different price points that you can choose from. The free option costs $0. Then there is a Pro option, you receive one brand kit and access to over 60 thousand templates and 4 million photos. Finally, the enterprise option, you will receive unlimited storage with this option as well as 24/7 support.

Earning Money Streaming Games

Yep….It is possible to make money playing games. A professional game streamer has the chance to show the world his/her capabilities and there are many people willing to pay to see that. As sometimes happens, this particular type of job has been labelled not serious at all" …or, "not a real job" but this is no different than any other professions and it should be viewed exactly the same. Is playing games your passion? Have a look at these platforms:

Twitch is the most popular way for professional game streamers. Twitch can provide its game streamers with income a few different ways. The first way is by receiving tips. These tips are payments from the streamers viewers and are paid at the viewer's decision. The second way it would be through subscriptions. A viewer will pay $5.00 per month and that fee is split between Twitch and the game streamer. This is more of a passive income; however, you will receive that money every month unless the subscriber cancels their subscription. The third way is through affiliate sales. When one of the viewers makes a purchase through an affiliate link the game streamer will earn a percentage of the money. The most important way for a game streamer to make an income off of Twitch is through internal sales funnel.

Driving-

Do you enjoy driving cars? Perhaps you don't want to spend all of your time online or in your living room. If that is the case don't worry, you can get paid to spend your days driving people around. There is no guarantee of how much money you are going to make on this, but the potential is there, and if you make the right choices, you can actually earn a substantial salary.

Uber - When you drive for Uber you will be able to make your own schedule, get paid every week automatically or you can use Instant Pay to get paid up to 5 times each day! You get to choose where you want to drive in the safest way possible because covered by Uber's auto insurance.

Lyft - If you choose to drive with Lyft, you can use their Direct Debit Card to get paid so you never have to wait for another direct deposit.

This account does not charge a fee and you will get cashback on all of your purchases including gas! Lyft allows unlimited payouts after every ride you provide. Lyft makes available mobile service vans that will come to you and provide maintenance for your vehicle where you are whenever you are available. Lyft also has a program for drivers without vehicles so that you can get on the road to earning right away.

Paid To Shop For Others

Getting paid to shop can be a dream job and it can be yours. There are companies that will pay you to go shopping for other people and deliver the products right to their door. You will receive orders right through the app. You can create your own schedule, meaning you work when you want and take off when you want. You can shop in the areas that you know, or you can expand your area and get to know new ones, allowing yourself to reach more customers. In order to get paid to shop you have to be at least 18 years old, a US citizen, have a smartphone, and the ability to lift 50 pounds.

InstaCart hires both full-service shoppers who deliver products to the customer's doors and they also hire in-store shoppers that will hand-select products for customers to pick up. You are paid through the app and can cash out your earnings when you need them.

Shipt- This is another company that hires people to shop for customers and deliver the products right to their door. According to the website, shoppers earn about $22 per hour and they are paid every week. You will need to be interviewed, and once you are approved, you can download the app and start earning.

Providing Care In Your Home

If you want to stay home all day and don't want to be on the internet, there are still options out there. According to Today, the average hourly rate for babysitting one child is about $16 per hour. If you are babysitting two children, you could make up to $19 an hour. Of course, the amount of money that you are going to make will depend on where you live and the hours that you are willing to work.

Don't want to babysit kids? You can also start a business creating a pet daycare right in your own home! There are a lot of people out there looking for someone to take care of their pets while they are away, and it could be you. What could be better than spending the day playing with balls of fluff?

If one of these sounds like a business that you are interested in, all you have to do is start letting your friends and family know about it or simply post an ad on social media. You can post fliers in your local grocery store as well. It is important for you to be prepared when you are taking on a business like this so make sure you have plenty of toys and the space needed before accepting clients.

Customer Service Representative

This is a great job for those who are good at talking on the phone while they are on their computer. Companies want workers who have excellent communication skills and are good with a computer to help their customers, resolve conflicts, place orders, find the correct sizes and answer customer questions. You can work full or part-time from home as a customer service representative. Most companies request that you are devoting your time in four-hour blocks.

VIP Desk- Has openings for remote customer service representatives. You will make between 9 and 14 dollars per hour working for VIP Desk. This is also a great company for those that are just starting out in the field.

LiveOps overs call center work in a variety of different fields. For example, you can take insurance claims, accept roadside assistance calls, take food orders, and so much more. Choose the field that works best for you. According to their website, you will make about 10 dollars per hour depending on the call volume, and the number of calls that are taken.

Online Tutor: Earn between $14 and $25 dollars per hour

You can work as an online tutor interacting with students via the internet. Most of the time you will be required to have a bachelor's degree in the subject that you are teaching. This can be a lucrative side job, or you can be an online tutor full time.

Tutor

Tutorvista

Tutorzilla

Marijuana License Checker

Cannabiz Media hires part-time researchers to collect and analyze information regarding marijuana licenses. They hire people who are located in Canada and the US.

Photography-

Do you love to take pictures? Did you know that your pictures can make you a lot of money online? Anyone with access to the internet and a computer can get paid to take stock photos! High-quality photos can sell for as much as $50 per image, and sometimes even more.

Companies That Buy Stock Photos:

500px

SmugMug Pro

Alamy

Chapter 6: Micro-jobs

Micro-Jobs-

MTurk allows you to make money online from the comfort of your own home doing whatever you want. You can do tasks such as edit text, data entry, rate pictures, and so much more. These are micro jobs that take about a few minutes to solve. Because these take so little time you will able to complete a lot of them in one day. Micro-jobs keep things interesting while allowing you to earn money from home

Taking Surveys

While there are not a lot of survey sites left that pay users to do that, there are a few you can rely on. Sitting down while you are watching television and completing a couple of surveys each evening is a great way to supplement your income. You can make as much as 15 dollars in 30 minutes taking paid surveys.

Harrispollonline

Watching Videos-

Inboxdollars

Lots of people love watching videos online. If this is the case, you may want to think about getting paid to watch a bunch of interesting things. There are quite a few companies out there that are willing to pay you to watch videos online.

You can get paid to watch movie trailers as well as advertisements for apps, taking pop quizzes about those videos, and much more.

Reviewing Music-

Slicethepie - Do you feel like you know a lot about music? Provide feedback for artists on their music as well as their other products that they offer such as clothing. Listen to tracks and write reviews for the artists to read. Building your reputation as a reviewer is going to allow you to earn more money. You can also earn money by referring your friends to sign up.

Playing Games-

Game Tester

Becoming a game tester allows you to make money doing what you love. You can work with developers that are creating new games. You will have to go through tests to ensure that you are capable of becoming a game tester and that your console is compatible with the games however, it is possible to make up to $150 an hour testing video games.

Earn Money Searching The Internet-

Swagbucks

Companies are willing to pay you to switch your search engine. Most people use Google whey they are searching the internet, but Google isn't paying you for that. Wouldn't you rather use a search engine that provides you with the same results while putting money in your pocket?

Read Emails-

Paid to read email

By simply signing up and allowing companies to send you emails you are going to be able to start making money from home. You will have to open the emails and click on a link however; this takes only a matter of seconds to do.

Completing Missions-

Mobeye

Going into stores and taking pictures of the product displays, checking their prices, and reviewing the promotions that are going are just a few ways to earn money completing missions. You are able to download the apps and see the list of missions near you. Once you book the task you will have 2 hours to complete it. This is a great way to earn money when you are out and about.

Uploading Receipts-

What do you do with all of your receipts after you have gone shopping? Chances are that you throw them away. Instead of throwing everything away, earn money from them. Ibotta and Fetch Rewards will pay you real money for uploading your receipt through their app.

Ibotta Provides rebates for items that you shop for every day. They pay directly through PayPal.

Fetch Rewards Pays you for every receipt that you upload. You earn points which are then turned into gift cards!

Using the Internet-

Computer Mobile Panel

You pay for the internet every month. Wouldn't it be nice if you got paid to use it? You can. By downloading a simple app and letting it run while you use the internet as you normally would you can start earning money. Companies are willing to pay for the information that they collect as you use the internet. They want to know all about what you are watching, listening to, buying, and searching for and they are willing to pay you for this information.

Watching Netflix-

Jobs Netflix

Netflix hires taggers to watch the shows and tag them. This allows Netflix to provide recommendations to their subscribers. The jobs are posted on the job board and are great for anyone who loves to binge-watch Netflix.

Viewing Ads On Your Phone-

By downloading apps on your phone, such as Slidejoy, you will be able to earn money every time you unlock your device. Small ads are played when you unlock your device. You can click the ad or skip it. Either way, you will still earn the same amount.

Test Apps-

App Coiner

Testing apps will help developers understand how they can improve the apps while also catching any glitches before they are released to the public. You will provide the developers with your opinion about the app, telling them what you enjoyed and what you think could be better. As you test the apps you will log all of the bugs that you find and once the task is completed you will be paid via PayPal.

Mystery Shopping-

ISecretShop

You can get paid to go into stores and be a secret shopper. Each job is going to pay differently depending on what you need to do but it is very easy for you to accept mystery shopping jobs through a variety of different apps allowing you to get make an income by simply shopping.

Creating Lists-

Listverse

You can make up to 100 dollars per 1500 word list that you create. These are 10 items lists, such as The Top 10 Ways Your Dog Shows You That They Love You, The Top 10 Ways To Save Money On Groceries, and so on.

Writing Reviews-

OnlineBookClub

People are able to receive free products for writing reviews all of the time. Wouldn't it be wonderful if we could get paid for writing reviews? Well, that is entirely possible. Online book club, for example, will provide you with a book to read and you will get paid between $5 and $60 per review you write.

Accepting Gigs-

GigWalk

By using mobile apps, you are able to see all of the different gigs available in your area. These could range from walking a dog to picking up milk at the grocery store, to going into a store and checking the displays. Gigs can take as few as 5 minutes or as long as a couple of hours. The pay ranges between 3 dollars to 100 dollars per gig, depending on how much time they will take.

Being a Friend-

Rent a Friend - Yes...some people are willing to pay for some company in exchange. You can be set your own hours, charge whatever you want to and work whenever you want to. You can earn around 50 dollars per hour while getting free meals, tickets to concerts as well as sporting events, and more all free. You get paid to hang out with people and be the friend that they really need.

Lose Weight-

My Achievement

People are willing to pay a lot of money to lose weight. They will purchase diet plans, pay for gym memberships and more. Wouldn't it be great if you could get paid to lose weight and get in shape? You can. There are plenty of apps out there that are willing to pay you to get healthy. These apps pay you for tracking your steps, the food that you eat, for participating in research studies and much more. If you want to get healthy why not get paid for it?

Create An Online Course-

Udemy

SkillShare

Do you have a skill that people are always asking you to teach them? If you do, it is possible for you to create an online course and get paid when people use it. One of the main reasons that people head to the internet is because they want to learn something. They may spend hours looking for the information that they need but if you are able to provide it to them in one spot, they are willing to pay for it.

Rent Out A Room-

AirBnB

Do you have a spare bedroom that you could start renting out to earn money from? Don't worry this doesn't mean that you have to get yourself a roommate unless of course, that is something that you want to do. The best way to earn money from your spare space would be to rent it out to travellers. Hosting allows you to charge as much as you want, rent out the room when you want and only accept who you want into your home. If you work through websites such as Airbnb, they will take care of the money and send you your payment through PayPal.

Participate in Market Research-

Adlerweiner

You can earn up to $100 per hour participating in market research such as focus groups. Companies want your opinion and they are willing to pay a lot for it. Participating in a focus group is very easy and it can be done in person or online. Some companies will ask you to test out a product before you participate in the group and some will just want you to tell them about your shopping habits for example.

Investing In The Stock Market-

Acorns

Stash

Investing in the stock market is a great way for you to earn money while you stay at home. Before you start investing in the stock market you will want to learn as much about it as you can. However, if you want to get started right away you can by using micro-investing. Today you can invest in the market without having to take the time to learn everything about it. There are apps that do all of the work for you and you can start out with as little as $5.00. Of course, try to take this seriously, letting an app taking care of your finances might not be a good idea, always make sure where you invest your money and try to consult a professional.

Teach-

If you wrote a course about your skill, you may also decide that you want to start teaching it locally as it has been done for ages. Many people learn better when they are taught one on one and if you are teaching an ability that they want to learn, you'll eventually find students on the way.

Become A Life Coach-

Have you ever dreamed of helping other people create the life that they always dreamed of? If you are able to interact with others, life coaches help people to make changes in their lives to improve their goals. You do not need any license to become a life coach and there are plenty of online courses that you can take completely free. As a life coach, you will listen to your client's problems and give them your advice, while helping them to see what variations they need to make.

Real-estate Investing-

FundRise

Becoming a real estate investor used to take thousands of dollars but today you can start investing in real estate for as little as 500 dollars. This works much like micro-investing except instead of investing in multiple stocks you are investing in multiple properties. Real estate investing can help you to diversify your portfolio and earn more money from home.

Blogging

While many people earn, a passive income blogging it is possible for you to start earning money with your blog by using affiliate links. You can sign up for an affiliate account with companies such as Amazon and use your blog to recommend products. When someone makes a purchase using your link, you will get paid.

Build Apps-

App

Did you know that 90% of the time that people spend on their mobile device is spent on apps? This means that there is a lot of opportunities for you building useful apps. While most apps are free, you can provide users with the opportunity to make in-app purchases. You can allow your users to make purchases through Apple or Google Pay. Of course, if you are creating an app that people are willing to pay for, you can charge an upfront fee. If you don't want to create your own app, you can pay some professional to do the job for you.

Product Testing-

Toluna

SurveyGizmo

Product testing is a fun way to make money online. There are plenty of websites out there that are willing to send you free products and pay you to test them. You can also find product testing jobs on social media. Sometimes a company will request that you purchase the product and get reimbursed for the purchase. While some companies feel that providing you with the free product is enough compensation, there are other companies that will pay big bucks to their product testers. Many people make the mistake of confusing these sites with survey sites, however, that is not what they are at all.

Online T-Shit Business-

Oberlo

Almost everyone wears t-shirts at one point or another. They are cheap and comfortable which means that you can earn a lot of money from them. If you can design your own t-shirts that will appeal to other people you may be able to create your own online t-shirt business. This is an extremely competitive business, so it is important that you are able to stand out. There are many different ways that you can have your t-shirts made. You can use a screen printer which is great for bulk orders or you can use heat transfer (iron-on) in order to place the images on t-shirts yourself. The good news is that you do not have to keep a huge supply of t-shirts in your home. You can choose a dropship supplier to take care of all of the orders for you.

Answer Questions-

Just Answer

Study Pool

Did you know that it is possible for you to make money online by answering questions? No. I am not talking about taking surveys. I am talking about earning an income by answering questions that real people have posted online. There are sites that are willing to pay you to provide their visitors with quality answers to their questions.

Travel Consultant-

Careers

Travel consultants make between $8,000 and $80,000 per year depending on how much they work, the number of clients that they have, and how much experience they have. Some people make huge amounts of money starting their own at home travel consultant business.

Complete Chores-

Taskrabbit

Everyone seems to have a to-do list that is a mile long and you can make tons of money completing other people's to-do list! From organizing closets to waiting in line to planning activities for kids or even taking care of the garden, there are hundreds of different types of tasks that you can get paid to complete. There are even people who have been able to make a couple of thousand dollars each WEEK by completing tasks for other people. You get to set your rates and you choose when you are going to work. The great thing about completing tasks is that you only have to do the jobs that you are interested in and have the skills for. If you know you won't enjoy a task you don't have to do it. Just bid on a different one.

Sell Lesson Plans-

Teachers pay teachers

Teachers are busy. They usually have way too many students to take care of, they are busy grading homework and often end up working late into the evening. This can leave them with very little time to create their lesson plans and that is where you can make a profit. Not only can you sell your lesson plans to teachers, but you can also sell them to homeschool parents who just don't have the time to come up with the plans on their own. This is a great idea for teachers who want to make some money on the side or for those who are no longer teaching but enjoy making lesson plans.

Sell Music-

Tunecore

If you are already writing and recording music, there is no reason that you should not get it out in front of your audience. So many people feel that they need an agent to accomplish with this, but times are changed and we live in an era where you can sell your music on your own. You can earn each time someone downloads one of your songs. Sure, that is not a lot of money when you are first starting out but as time goes by and you find yourself with more and more fans, you could be raking in a lot of dough.

Edit Videos-

Viedit

Today video editing is extremely important. Many YouTubers rely on other people to edit their videos so that they can focus on other details to ensure their channel becomes popular. You can cash in on this. When you spend your day in front of the camera chances are that you do not want to spend your evening editing videos which is why this industry is booming! Of course, you can always use freelancing platforms to find video editing jobs as well which is a great way for you to ensure that you are able to decide how much you want to make as well as how many projects you want to complete.

Chapter 7: At Home Businesses

Not all work at home jobs are online. If you don't want to work for another company online or you want to start your own business at home, don't worry, it is possible. Not only is it potential for you to start your own in-home business but people actually do it every day.

Tons of hugely successful businesses began as an in-home business and most of the time the startup costs are much less.

The first thing that you have to do is to come up with a business idea. In this chapter, you will find lots of different clues. Of course, there are hundreds if not thousands of other careers that you can start from your basement. This list is just to give you a hint of what you could do if your mind is drawing a blank.

What you choose to start should be something that you are passionate about. It should be something that you are going to enjoy doing and that you are knowledgeable about. If you plan on learning something new, it is going to take more time than if you focused on the skills you already have, but sure it will be worth the effort.

The next thing that you will want to think about is your target market. If you do not know your target market or are not reaching them, your business will not succeed. I recently started an at-home business selling products. I created the social media page, invited all of my friends and started posting the product for sale. I made one sale in one week. I was discouraged. However, when I focused on reaching my target market, I started making sales faster than I could keep up. As soon as I post an item for sale, someone is buying it. That is the difference that knowing your target market makes.

It is also important for you to know who your competitors are. By knowing about your opponents, you are going to be able to stand out from the crowd and be as unique as possible.

Before you roll out your business you want to test your idea. You can do this by testing it on your friends and family. Before I started my business, I took a few of my products and offered them for sale on my personal social media page. When I found out that they would sell quickly I knew my business would be a success.

Once you introduce your business to the public, the best thing that you can do is work part-time running your business from your home.

Being an entrepreneur comes with risk. If you are currently employed it is best to start your business in your free time and then when it grows, focus on it full-time.

Determine how much you need to make in order to decide how much you are going to work. Know how much money you need to make each week in order for you to make the profit that you desire. For example, for my business, I work one day each week. I post my products for sale, earn my money and the rest of the week, I don't think about it. Knowing how much you need or want to make will allow you to create a schedule that works best for you.

If you are starting home-based commerce, you may want to consider opening a business bank account. This account is going to allow you to keep your business money separate from your personal money. It will also allow you to track any spending as well as what you earn.

Even if you have no money to start your business there are at home service-based jobs you can create. Earn the money that you need and start the career that you have always dreamed of.

Selling handmade products-

Most people already know that you can sell your handmade products on Etsy or Ebay, however, there are so many other places for you to sell your product. Starting a social media page for your business should be your first priority. You will want to invite all of your friends and family to like the page and then they can invite their friends and so on. Here you will post the products that you are selling. You will also want to sell them on marketplace groups that you belong to on social media as well. This is a great way for you to let people know about your product. Of course, you can create a website that people can order products from when your business is big enough.

What types of handmade products can you sell? There are plenty of options out there and you don't have to worry if someone is already selling what you want to make. Work to make your product the best, present it well, and you will have plenty of customers.

- Jewellery
- Paintings
- Wood burnings

- Soaps
- Candles
- Bath Bombs
- Lotions
- Fishing Flies
- Woodwork
- Hair bows
- Pillows
- Rugs
- Anything crocheted
- Quilts and other blankets
- Bath Salts (Yes, the ones that go in the bathtub)
- Exfoliating scrubs
- Scarfs

- Headbands

- Tumblers

- And any other craft that you can create!

People go crazy for handmade items. If you enjoy making things by hand you can sell them and earn a lot of money doing so. If you are making body products, you could consider using only organic ingredients which will increase your sales dramatically.

Flipping products-

This another way to make money that many people never think of. You can head out to your local resale shops or garage sales and if you have a good eye, turn a huge profit selling products online. For example, I was able to purchase a Coach purse in perfect condition for 4 dollars, which I later sold for 48 dollars online. I knew what I was looking for I was able to make a huge profit. You can do the same thing.

If you have a good eye for brand name clothing, antiques, or other items that people are always on the lookout for, this could be a great business for you to start out of your home. Be sure that you do have room to store your items though because sometimes they do not sell as quickly as you had hoped. Lots of people make a great living flipping the items that they find at local thrift stores. You can as well.

Become a personal trainer!

If you love fitness and you love seeing people get healthy this might be the perfect job for you. You can choose to take on clients in your own home, or you can create a Bootcamp where you will instruct many clients at the same time. Simply setting up a morning Bootcamp to help people get in shape can end up having lots of clients sign up which means lots of money in your pocket and satisfaction.

Cooking/Baking-

Do you love to cook? If you are one of those people who can spend hours in the kitchen creating amazing masterpieces, this may be the business for you. Spend your time cooking and sell those meals to people in your area who do not have time to cook but are sick of fast food. Providing healthy well-balanced meals is a great way to earn income right from your home. If you love to bake, you can sell your baked goods as well. It always amazes me how quickly these products sell out! Homemade bread, muffins, cakes, pies, and other products will sell faster than you can get them out of the oven! If you are great at decorating cakes, you could also offer that service as well.

Gift Basket Designing-

Do you have the ability to spot a deal a mile away? Many people who are able to find great deals on products create gift baskets and sell them online. These are huge sellers during the holidays and sell great all year long. You can grab some cheap 1 dollar baskets at your local dollar store and fill them with products that you get on sale. People are willing to pay a lot of money for these gift baskets if they look good! You can also post them online, creating your own shop to sell them in. If you make your own products to sell this is a great way to sell a lot of products at one time.

Party Planner-

If you have the ability to put together great parties, this might be the perfect business for you. You will need to be very organized and have great customer service skills, as well as the willingness to get out and meet new people. You will need to know a little about marketing as well. Remember though that you are not just competing with any other party planners that you come across but local facilities as well as restaurants so you must provide excellent work while adding a personal touch to your parties.

Teaching Music-

Most kids who attend public school are going to take some sort of music program at some point. However, that is usually the extent of their exposure to music. As they grow older, they may find that they want to become more musical, learn how to sing, or play an instrument. If you have the ability to teach children or adults how to sing or play an instrument you could be making a decent amount of money from your home.

There is a big market for music teachers! You will need to be very firm on your policies, the pricing as well as what happens if they cancel. It would be best for you to make sure that you use your home to teach the lessons instead of having to travel to your students.

Cleaning Houses-

Sure, with this job you have to leave your house on occasion, but you are still considered home-based, aren't you? You will be running your housecleaning service out of your own home. This is a more obvious idea when it comes to starting a new at-home business, but it is also one that many people overlook. Cleaning can be hard work but if it is something that you enjoy, you can spend your time doing it and earning. People who are great cleaners are going to be able to pick up new clients very quickly. The most important thing that you will have to know is how to clean well. You will also have to consider the services that you are willing to provide. Are you willing to do laundry? Dishes? Deep cleaning? Or do you want to focus on light housework? All of this will affect the amount that you can charge.

Gardening-

Did you know that you can make money growing food and selling it in your local community? The type of fruit or vegetables that you will grow is going to depend on the growing environment that you have available to you, but you can make a living during the harvest season by selling what you grow. You will make even more money if it is all organically grown. Selling the products from your home, online, or at the local farmers market is going to bring you a nice income. In the spring, you can sell seedlings to other local farmers or gardeners who don't have time to grow the plants themselves. You may also choose, if you have a large garden, to hold "pick your own" events where people come to garden, pick what they want and pay you a specific price. Of course, this is not going to provide you with an income all year, but it can help during the warmer months. It may also provide you with the option to work a few months out of the year and take the rest of the time off.

Aromatherapy-

It is possible for you to start your own aromatherapy business. You can sell your products online if you choose, creating your own store. Knowledge about essential oils and how to mix them is required. Of course, you will need to look into your packaging supplies, marketing tactics, and so on but if you are willing to invest your time and a little money you can create a very profitable business out of your home.

Computer Repair-

Almost everyone owns a computer today and that means that almost everyone has to deal with computer problems. If you are knowledgeable about computers as well as how to fix them, you can create your own computer repair business. Of course, you will have to work to get your name known and get your first customers, but it is like that with every business. If you are providing your customers with quality work, they will start telling their friends about you and you will have more work than you know what to do with. Make sure that you have a workspace that is dedicated to that. Today, starting a computer repair business is easier than ever because you can market your business on the internet, starting a social media page, or a website!

Handyman-

Are you really good at fixing things? Do you enjoy working with your hands? Starting your own handyman business might be for you. I have personally known people who have done this and make at least 50 dollars per hour doing what they love. They are in demand and never have to go out looking for work. Make sure that you have the right tools and any license that your area requires. If you have all of this, you are ready to get started going out and putting bids in on projects. Before you know it, customers are going to be calling you asking you to bid on their jobs.

Lawn Service-

Providing lawn care allows you to spend your days outside doing something that you enjoy. In years past, this was not as great of a business to get into because we had teenagers going door to door offering to mow lawns for very little money. Today that does not happen. People struggle to find the time to take care of their lawns the way that they want to. If you have the skills to provide people with well-manicured lawns for a price that is affordable you may want to consider starting this. Don't only advertise to homeowners though, talk to landlords who need their properties lawns kept up, real estate agents who need to ensure that the lawns on their properties are appealing, as well as other businesses. In the fall, offer leaf removal services. In the winter offer snow removal services. You can keep yourself busy all year long or only work in the spring, summer, and fall months, allowing yourself the rest in the winter for some different project.

Pet Training-

We live in a world where everyone is so busy. Hardly anyone has the time to train their pets anymore but that does not stop us from keeping them around. If you are able to train pets effectively this could be the perfect business for you. Some people may want you to potty train their puppies or kittens. Others may want you to teach their pets tricks. If you can do this, you can charge quite a bit of money. You see, pets are not something that people want to skimp on. They are willing to pay a pretty penny when it comes to their pets and you can cash in on this.

Professional Organizer-

Are you really good at organizing? Do you enjoy spending your days getting everything organized and tidy? I bet you already know that there are tons of people out there who are not quite as organized as they want to be. You can help them out by being a professional organizer. You can charge by the hour or by the room. You can choose to do all of the organization completely on your own or you can offer a service to help people become more organized, teaching them the skill as the two of you attack the area together.

Motivational Speaking-

Have you ever sat back while listening to motivational speakers and found yourself wishing that you could make a living doing that? Motivational speakers earn a lot of money for sharing their knowledge. Have a hard time speaking in front of a crowd? Don't worry, this is a skill that you can learn. The hardest part about becoming a motivational speaker is getting booked. While it may take you a little while to get your name out there, once you have, chances are that you will start getting requests from all over from people who want to hear you speak. Do you have a story to tell? People want to hear it and they are willing to pay if you are willing to tell it to them.

Starting your own at home business is a great way for you to finally be able to earn money from doing what you love. You don't have to dread going to work every day and you no longer have to allow your job to cause you misery.

Before you commit on your own at home business you will want to check your state as well as city requirements. Some will allow you to start any business out of your home without limitations however, there are other's that require you to get a license.

Your business is only going to be as strong as the foundation that it is built upon. Once you launch your rocket, you will want to focus on growing your customer base and making the right financial decisions. Start small but dream big!

Spotting Scams

While scams are not new in human history, technology has given us way too many possibilities of being scammed. Peculiar, subtle frauds are constantly arising and evolving, not easy to realize but not impossible. You will see ads like, "Make $4,000 a Week Working From Home Filling Out Forms," or "Make $10,000 a Month Working From Home Stuffing Envelopes."

So many people fall for these scams because they desire a better life, and they want to make a lot of money fast. I will tell you that none of the jobs that I talked about in this guide are get-rich quick schemes. These are all legitimate jobs where you will need to apply seriously; there is no shortcut but get your self in, no magic button or miracle. When you see a job that sounds like it is too good to be true, remind yourself that it is and better check twice.

Another way that people get scammed when they are trying to become an at-home worker is by paying to work. You should never have to pay someone in order to work for someone! Of course, there are fees on freelancing job boards depending on what package you want, but this is fair enough and essential, and you could use the free package too and do fine at the beginning. Always check at the source, make sure you read contracts, policies, try to avoid what you cannot fully understand and don't give your personal information to unknown companies.

There are tons of scams out there. That is why I have provided you with the information in this book, to ensure that you do not get caught up in one of them. I am not telling you any of this to discourage you but instead to make you aware that there are people out there who will try to take advantage of your desire to change.

This can be extremely difficult to deal with if you are having financial problems due to being unemployed or switching jobs. The best options would be for you to only accept work that is willing to pay through companies such as PayPal or similar. This way you know that your money is protected.

When you arm yourself with the right information and you put in the time to learn about the jobs that are available to you, you will find that becoming self-employed can be a breeze. I suggest that you do your own research once you have decided what industry you want to work in. In this book, I have provided a short description of the different jobs that are out there as well as a link to an example of the job. The information that I have provided is minimal for each job. Please do not allow one short paragraph to determine what type of job you want to do from home. Instead, take some time and look into the jobs that interest you. A simple Google search will provide you with all sorts of information about each job, the requirements, as well as the average pay, minimum earnings, and maximum earnings, as they might change overtime.

Learning more about the topic that you are interested in will give you a much better idea of what each job entails, and it will help you to make a more informed decision. Most importantly, never rush into remote work.

Becoming an at-home worker is a huge decision to make. With it comes many changes that you will have to get used to. In the beginning, you probably are not going to have as much work as someone who has been freelancing for 10 years which is why it is important to keep your day job if at all possible. Slowly move into working remotely full-time as your finances allow you to.

Thanks for reading this book, please consider leaving a quick review on Amazon and help to support my work. Thanks! .

Conclusion

Working from home allows you to be your own boss. No longer are you going to have someone assigning work to you that you do not want to do or telling you what to do with your time. You will never have to worry about showing up late for work again or asking for time off. When you work remotely, no one is going to be looking over your shoulder or telling you how they would have done the work. You never have to worry about clichés trying to get you fired or office gossip.

Far too often, people find themselves feeling that they are stuck in their job. Every day they do the same thing over and over again. They go to the same office and they do the same type of work. When you work at home though you have the ability to mix things up. You can, for example, write books three days a week, transcribe audio one day a week, and edit videos on a different day. This helps to keep the excitement flowing and keeps you interested in what you are doing.

Even more importantly when you become a freelancer you have the ability to grow. You will begin to see more opportunities open up to you. Finally, you will have the time to spend studying and learning that new skill you always wanted to learn. You will be able to keep up with the latest trends ensuring that you are providing your clients with the most up to date product possible. You can even expand your business as you learn new ways.

It is important for you to think realistically, Many people think of themselves curled up on the sofa with a cup of coffee as Netflix plays their favourite television show, as they imagine easily completing all of their work.

While working at home is a wonderful job and it is very enjoyable it is still a job and it has to be treated as such. It is perfectly fine to curl up on the sofa on the days when you are feeling under the weather and it is a great benefit of becoming a freelancer, to be able to work anywhere that you like, however, you do not want to get too comfortable. Getting too comfortable can mean that you are forgetting just how important your priorities are.

When you learn how to balance yourself, you will focus much more on what you need to get done while still having plenty of free time to spend with your family. You will also find that you are able to retain your clients while working the hours that you choose to work.

It is a good idea to spend some time thinking about how you are going to maintain your focus, there are tons of distractions out there all of them fighting for your attention.

Working from home comes with its challenges but many people find that the benefits far outweigh the effort. The truth is that no matter what job we choose to do, we are going to be faced with difficulties, which are indispensable steps toward success.

CYRIL EVERILL

www.ingramcontent.com/pod-product-compliance
Lightning Source LLC
Chambersburg PA
CBHW071416210526
45465CB00001B/418